Multicooker Mira

Your Multicooker Recipe Collection

BY

MOLLY MILLS

License Notes

No part of this book may be copied, replicated, distributed, sold or shared without the express and written consent of the Author.

The ideas expressed in the book are for entertainment purposes. The Reader assumes all risk when following any guidelines and the Author accepts no responsibility if damages occur due to actions taken by the Reader.

Table of Contents

Introduction

It is safe to impress the multicooker as a miracle cooker. It can do so much when you tinker with the different settings. You can boil/steam, sauté, deep-fry, stew, roast, and slow cook with a simple touch of the dial. You just have to prepare your ingredients, have your recipe on hand, and be ready to follow the steps to become a multicooker goddess. But of course, you need recipes on hand. This is what this cookbook is made for. We have 30 of the best things you can make with your multicooker so you can put it into real good use. Care to take a sneak peek at our listing?

Here it is:

- Steamed Spiced Potatoes
- Bean Ham Soup
- Creamy Chicken Risotto
- Steamed Salmon with Salsa Verde
- Multicooker Shrimp Boil
- Multicooker Barbacoa Tacos
- Mexican Pork Stew
- Mac Cheese with Ham Peas
- Multicooker Pancake
- Peanut Chicken Ramen
- Multicooker Peach Cobbler
- Tasty Butter Chicken
- Southern Fish Fry
- Multicooker Corned Beef
- Multicooker Rotisserie Chicken
- Farrotto
- Multicooker BBQ Ribs
- Multicooker Beef Bourguignon
- Chicken Noodle Soup
- Multicooker Cabbage Rolls
- Cottage Cheese Pudding
- Corn and Potato Chowder
- Chickpea Curry
- Cheesy Egg and Sausage Casserole
- Multicooker Korean Beef

- Beef and Mushroom Stew
- Multicooker Fish Mix
- Multicooker Spaghetti
- Multicooker Pork Chops
- Garlicky Pot Roast

We are out to prove that the multicooker is a miracle maker. Through this recipe collection, you can turn from a novice cook to a super amazing one – because yeah, you can practically make anything!

What's in A Multicooker?

The multicooker is an amazing kitchen innovation we can all find useful. With it around, you will not have a problem concocting even the most complicated recipes. It offers multiple benefits that will allow you to perform a handful of cooking tasks, which you traditionally need different kitchen utensils for.

But just like anything, not all multicookers are made the same. Some are more superior to others, with astounding features every home cook can only dream about. While it is safe to say that all multicookers are amazing, you should also pay close attention to the user manual of the unit you are looking to purchase and make sure it meets your needs and preferences right.

Basically, a multicooker is composed of a housing complete with a safe-locking lid, an inner pot, a heating element, a control panel that reveals its multiple functions, a digital display, a timer and temperature sensor, and a digital display that provides information about where you are in the cooking process. Other units may have more impressive features or may be equipped with a bigger capacity but such difference also reflects on the price tag. To be wise, make sure that you are getting the most value for every cent that you pay for. That could be enough to tell you are making a good purchase.

Here are some features you might want to take note of:

- The size – Size matters, of course. You would want a multicooker size that's big enough to keep up with the size of your family meals but compact enough to eat as little space at the kitchen counter as possible.
- The design – There is an assortment of multicooker designs available in the market. It would be nice to find one that is on the same color theme or style as the rest of the items in your counter. So, everything looks lovely.
- The function – When all is said and done, how well the multicooker performs still reigns supreme. You have to check on its function, durability, cooking abilities, and overall quality. Check out user comments and recommendations because those will be your best reference to the best unit or brand out in the market today.

Once you found the unit that fits your preferences and your budget, it's time to fire it up and get started. The multicooker offers endless possibilities. You just need this useful cookbook to guide you in concocting yummy recipes for the entire family. So, without further ado, let's go!

Steamed Spiced Potatoes

If you want to make a quick side dish without getting your hand too involved, this is the recipe for you. It may look like simple boiled potatoes at first sight, but you could make it great, definitely. Your choice of spices and herbs to liven up the dish will be your secret weapons. This is one of the simplest things that should get you going with the multicooker. It's a wonderful start, to say the least.

Serving Size: 4

Prep Time: 37 mins

Ingredients:

- 1 ½ lbs. old potatoes, peeled and cut inti 2-inch pieces
- 1 tbsp fresh parsley, chopped
- 4 pcs chives, chopped
- 1 tbsp extra virgin olive oil
- 2 cups cold water
- Salt and pepper to taste

Instructions:

1. Put enough water in the multicooker, then, arrange the steam bowl. Make sure the water does not touch the steam bowl.

2. Toss potatoes with a bit of salt and pepper. Pour onto the steam bowl.

3. Cover the lid and switch the multicooker on. Let the potatoes cook for about 25 minutes, then, switch to "keep warm"

4. When ready to serve, toss potatoes with oil, parsley, and chives, plus more salt and pepper as needed.

Bean Ham Soup

Beans are some of the best things that work well with the multicooker. Why, cooking the beans in this miracle worker will cut short your waiting time. That's because you can skip soaking the beans in water overnight. You can start with your dry beans and enjoy them soft and tasty at the end of the cooking time. This soup is perfect for rainy days. It will liven up your spirit with its comforting taste. And please, don't omit the magic of a can of pork and beans added afterward. It adds a unique layer to this already mouthwatering dish.

Serving Size: 6

Prep Time: 1 hr. 10 mins

Ingredients:

- 1-16oz can pork and beans, undrained
- 2 cups dry navy beans
- 1 cup ham, chopped
- 2 pcs carrots, chopped
- 2 pcs celery stalks, chopped
- 1 pc onion, chopped
- 1-14.5oz can diced tomatoes, undrained
- 2 cups chicken broth
- 2 cups water
- Salt and freshly ground black pepper to taste

Instructions:

1. Combine all the ingredients in a multicooker, except for ham, and the pork and beans in a can.

2. Stir to blend, then, close the lid, tightly sealed.

3. Turn the multicooker to "Manual" and set to pressure cook for about 45 minutes. Release pressure afterward.

4. Stir in ham and pork and beans and adjust seasoning as needed before serving.

Creamy Chicken Risotto

Just like the beans, risotto works great with the multicooker. The dish simply comes out creamier and tastier. For this recipe, we are experimenting with some bold flavors, including Cajun and green tea, and the result is truly impressive. Try it!

Serving Size: 8

Prep Time: 30 mins

Ingredients:

- 2 cups Arborio rice
- 1 lb. boneless and skinless chicken thighs, sliced into chunks
- 8oz Andouille sausage, sliced diagonally
- 1 ½ cups multicolored bell peppers, diced
- 6 green tea bags
- 1 ½ cups onions, diced
- 1 cup green onions, sliced
- 2 tbsp Cajun seasoning
- 1 tsp ground coriander
- 1 tbsp garlic salt
- 2 tbsp extra virgin olive oil
- 3 cups water

Instructions:

1. Stir together Cajun seasoning, coriander, and garlic salt.

2. Sprinkle about a tablespoon of dry marinade onto chicken and toss to coat, reserve the remaining seasoning mix.

3. Turn on the multicooker to "Manual" and heat oil on medium.

4. Brown chicken for about 3 minutes, stirring occasionally.

5. Stir in onions and cook for another 3 minutes.

6. Add green tea and water and boil.

7. Mix in rice, sausage, bell peppers, and the remaining seasoning mix.

8. Close the lid tightly and place the cooker on full pressure at high heat.

9. Set the timer for 5 minutes, release the pressure, and let it stand for another 5 minutes.

10. Remove the teabags and discard.

11. Serve with a garnish of freshly chopped green onions.

Steamed Salmon with Salsa Verde

Steaming is a great way to prepare fish. It keeps the fish flaky but not dry. And yes, you can do this recipe with a multicooker. Every unit comes with a steamer tray where you can lay the salmon fillet and cook for about 5 minutes. Take the Salsa Verde from the fridge or make your own, then, dinner is ready!

Serving Size: 4

Prep Time: 15 mins

Ingredients:

- Kosher salt and freshly ground black pepper to taste
- 4 pcs salmon fillets
- 1 cup salsa verde
- 1 tbsp olive oil

Instructions:

1. Add about 2 inches deep of water to the multicooker and then, the steamer basket, greased with olive oil, on top. Make sure the water does not touch the steamer basket.

2. Sprinkle some salt and pepper on salmon fillets and arrange them at the steamer basket.

3. Set the cooker on steam setting, close the lid, and let it cook for about 5 minutes.

4. Transfer salmon to a serving platter with a bowl of salsa verde on the side.

Multicooker Shrimp Boil

It's always nice to have a seafood fest and it's incredibly nicer that you can make a dish for it at your multicooker. Here is everybody's favorite seafood boil, which you can make for your summer parties and outdoor barbecues in under 10 minutes. How impressive is that?

Serving Size: 6

Prep Time: 35 mins

Ingredients:

- 2 tbsp fresh parsley leaves, chopped
- 1 ½ lbs. medium shrimps
- 1 pc lemon, cut into wedges
- 3 ears corn, halved and cut into three parts
- 1 ½ lbs. baby red potatoes
- ½ pc sweet onion, chopped
- 3 garlic cloves, minced
- 1-12.8oz package smoked Andouille sausage, thinly sliced
- 4 tsp Old Bay seasoning, divided
- 1-16oz pilsner beer
- 1 tbsp hot sauce
- ¼ cup unsalted butter

Instructions:

1. Stir together sausages, potatoes, onions, hot sauce, and 3 teaspoons Old Bay seasoning in a multicooker.

2. Scatter corn and then, pour beer.

3. Close the lid and select "Manual". Set the pressure on high heat and the timer at 5 minutes. Then, release the pressure.

4. Stir in shrimp and set the pressure to high again and let cook for another minute. Release the pressure again.

5. Meanwhile, melt butter in a pan over medium fire and sauté garlic until lightly browned. Sprinkle with remaining seasoning and stir for about a minute.

6. Transfer shrimps mixture in a serving bowl, drizzle with butter and garlic mix, and garnish with parsley. Serve with lemon wedges on the side.

Multicooker Barbacoa Tacos

The multicooker is most useful for dishes where you need to tenderize tough cuts of meat and then translate it into a delicious treat. That's exactly what this dish is all about. We have super tender beef shredded to make a delightful treat stuffed into corn tortillas. Normally, this would take long hours of simmering or slow cooking but with the multicooker, all you need is a little over an hour and finish.

Serving Size: 6

Prep Time: 1 hr. 10 mins

Ingredients:

- 6in corn tortillas
- 2 ½ lbs. boneless beef chuck, trimmed and sliced into chunks
- 1 cup pico de gallo
- 1 cup Cotija cheese, shredded
- 3 garlic cloves, minced
- 1 pc chipotle chili in adobo, minced
- ½ cup chicken broth
- 2 tbsp vegetable oil
- 2 pcs bay leaves
- 2 tbsp fresh lime juice
- ¼ cup apple cider vinegar
- 2 tsp dried oregano
- ¼ tsp ground cloves
- 2 tsp ground cumin
- 1 tsp salt
- ½ tsp freshly ground black pepper

Instructions:

1. Stir together lime juice, vinegar, garlic, chili, oregano, cloves, cumin, salt, and pepper in a bowl. Set aside.

2. Set the multicooker on sauté and adjust the button to select high heat.

3. Heat oil in the pot and brown beef chunks, stirring occasionally, for 8 minutes.

4. Pour in the lime juice mixture and broth, then, stir in bay leaves.

5. Close the lid and seal tightly, then, set on Manual/Pressure Cook and the timer for 30 minutes. Release the pressure and open the lid.

6. Remove the bay leaves and discard and transfer beef to a chopping board. Let it cool a little then, use two forks to shred the meat.

7. To assemble, divide the meat between the tortillas, spoon over pico de gallo, and garnish with cheese.

8. Serve and enjoy.

Mexican Pork Stew

Oh, did we mention that the multicooker is perfect for stews? It is! In fact, you can forget about all the complications and hard work of preparing a stew if you have a handy multicooker at home. This Mexican Pork Stew, traditionally known as Pozole, is a nice way to stew in the cooker. It's a delicious, full-pack dish with loads of meaty and peppery flavors.

Serving Size: 6

Prep Time: 1 hr. 5 mins

Ingredients:

- 1 tsp ground cumin
- 1 tbsp lime juice
- 2 pcs yellow onions, chopped
- 2 ½ lbs. boneless pork shoulder, sliced into 2-inch chunks
- 4 cloves garlic, minced
- ½ cup cilantro, chopped
- 1 tsp dried oregano
- ½ tsp ground coriander
- 2-15oz cans hominy, drained and rinsed
- 1 pc cinnamon stick
- 1 pc chipotle pepper in adobo, minced
- 1 tbsp smoked paprika
- 2 tsp chili powder
- 2 pcs Poblano peppers, seeded and diced
- 4 cups chicken broth
- 2 tbsp vegetable oil
- 1 tsp salt, divided
- 1 tsp ground black pepper, divided
- 1-12oz can lager-style beer

Instructions:

1. Sprinkle pork chunks with half of the salt and half of the pepper.

2. Set the multicooker to "sauté" and set on high heat.

3. Add oil and brown pork for about 3 minutes, stirring often. Remove from the pot and transfer to a bowl.

4. Stir in onions, garlic, peppers, cinnamon, oregano, cumin, coriander, paprika, and chili powder into the pot until fragrant.

5. Return pork to the pot, pour beer and chicken stock, and hit "cancel".

6. Close the lid tightly, press "manual", and set the timer to 35 minutes. Turn off the cooker and release the pressure.

7. Stir in hominy and lime juice, then, sprinkle the remaining salt and pepper.

8. Garnish with chopped cilantro before serving.

Mac Cheese with Ham Peas

The multicooker offers endless pasta-abilities. And everybody's favorite Mac and Cheese is one of the best things you could make with it. But no, this is not your ordinary Mac and Cheese. We also added some ham and peas to make it extra appetizing and wonderful. Let's start cooking!

Serving Size: 6

Prep Time: 50 mins

Ingredients:

- 1-16oz package elbow macaroni
- 1 cup Monterey Jack cheese, shredded
- 2 cups cheddar cheese, shredded
- 1 cup cooked ham, diced
- ½ cup peas
- 1 tsp hot sauce
- 1-12oz can evaporated milk
- ⅓ cup whole milk
- 2 tbsp unsalted butter
- 4 cups water
- 1 tsp dry mustard powder
- Salt and freshly ground black pepper to taste

Instructions:

1. Stir together macaroni, about a tablespoon of salt, mustard powder, hot sauce, and water in a multicooker.

2. Close the lid and set on "manual" and on high pressure.

3. Let it cook for about 10 minutes and release the pressure accordingly.

4. Switch the function to "sauté" and on low heat, then, pour milk, evaporated milk, and butter.

5. Add ham, peas, and cheeses. Sprinkle with some salt and pepper and stir to blend.

6. Serve and enjoy.

Multicooker Pancakes

Want some fluffy pancakes? Your multicooker can provide for that. You can have a super fluffy and ultimately delicious version of this breakfast staple and mind you; it would not need any flipping! This is a great recipe when you are feeding such a large appetite. Its size and taste would surely suffice.

Serving Size: 8

Prep Time: 55 mins

Ingredients:

- 2 cups all-purpose flour
- 2 tsp baking powder
- 2 tbsp granulated sugar
- 1 tsp Kosher salt
- 2 tbsp maple syrup
- 1 tbsp butter
- 1 ½ cups milk
- 2 pcs large eggs
- Cooking spray

Instructions:

1. Combine all the ingredients except for the butter and maple syrup until the batter is smooth.

2. Lightly grease the inner pot and pour the batter.

3. Set the multicooker to "slow cook" and the timer to 45 minutes.

4. Carefully remove the pancake from the pan, serve with cut butter on top and drizzled with maple syrup.

Peanut Chicken Ramen

Ramen is so comforting. And this special recipe will surely warm you up during those cold nights. It's Thai-inspired, infused with peanut butter and some spices, plus chicken and veggies and of course, the noodles. It's such a lovely treat in every spoonful, starting from the flavor-packed soup to the rest of the ingredients. And since you are doing it in the multicooker, it should be ready in about half an hour.

Serving Size: 6

Prep Time: 30 mins

Ingredients:

- 10oz ramen noodles
- ¾ lb. boneless and skinless chicken breasts
- 2 pcs red bell peppers, seeded and chopped
- 8oz cremini mushrooms, sliced
- 1 tbsp fresh ginger, peeled and grated
- 1 garlic clove, minced
- 3 cups fresh baby spinach
- 1/3 cup fresh cilantro, roughly chopped
- ¼ cup roasted peanuts, chopped
- 1 tbsp toasted sesame oil
- 1/3 cup creamy peanut butter
- ¼ cup Thai red curry paste
- 1-14oz can coconut milk
- Juice of 1 lime
- ¼ cup soy sauce
- 2 tbsp fish sauce
- 2 tbsp honey
- 4 cups chicken broth

Instructions:

1. Stir together chicken, red bell peppers, mushrooms, ginger, garlic, peanut butter, coconut milk, curry paste, soy sauce, fish sauce, honey and chicken broth in the multicooker pot.

2. Secure the lid, then, set on high heat and the timer for 10 minutes. Release the pressure to release the steam and switch to "sauté".

3. Transfer chicken to a chopping board and shred using two forks.

4. Put chicken back to the pot together with the noodles, spinach, cilantro, and lime juice.

5. Set the timer on for 5 minutes until the noodles are cooked.

6. Ladle soup onto serving bowls, sprinkle with more freshly chopped cilantro, plus roasted peanuts and a drizzle of toasted sesame oil.

7. Serve warm.

Multicooker Peach Cobbler

The multicooker is as good with your desserts as they are with your sides and mains. This Peach Cobbler recipe is a wonderful reason to tinker with your unit and make it work. The idea of being able to cook this dish without an oven and in less than half an hour that is really something you could praise the multicooker for.

Serving Size: 5

Prep Time: 30 mins

Ingredients:

- 8pcs fresh peaches, sliced
- 2 cups +2 tbsp all-purpose flour
- 1 ½ tsp baking powder
- 2 tbsp cornstarch
- 1 tsp salt
- 2 ¼ cups white sugar, divided
- 1 tsp lemon juice
- 8 tbsp butter
- 1 cup buttermilk
- ½ cup water

Instructions:

1. Stir together peaches, 2 tablespoons of flour, cornstarch, 1 and ½ cups sugar, and lemon juice in a bowl until well blended.

2. Place water on the multicooker pot, switch on the unit to "sauté" and let the water boil.

3. Stir in the peaches mixture and let it soften.

4. Meanwhile, mix together the remaining sugar, flour, baking powder, and salt.

5. Fold in the butter and mix, then, add buttermilk.

6. Add the flour mixture into the peaches, a spoonful at a time, close the lid, and switch to "manual". Set on high pressure and the timer to 20 minutes.

7. Release the pressure and spoon the peach cobbler into the serving bowl. Add a scoop of vanilla ice cream per serving.

Tasty Butter Chicken

Butter Chicken is a delicious recipe that is perfect for the multicooker. Why, it becomes moist and tasty when treated at a miracle worker and makes for a great dish that prepares in only 15 minutes. If you are thinking about a quick and easy dinner, you should not go very far.

Serving Size: 6

Prep Time: 15 mins

Ingredients:

- 6 pcs boneless and skinless chicken thighs, cubed
- 1 tbsp ginger, chopped
- ½ pc onion
- 1 tbsp garlic, minced
- 1 ½ cups heavy cream
- 1 ½ cups tomato sauce
- 3 tsp garam masala
- 1 ½ tsp chili powder
- 1 ½ tsp cumin
- 5 tbsp butter
- 2 tbsp cornstarch, dissolved in
- ¼ cup water

Instructions:

1. Switch on the pressure cooker to "sauté" and melt butter on the multicooker pot.

2. Add onions and chicken into the pot and stir often.

3. Add the rest of the ingredients, except for the cornstarch and water, and mix well.

4. Secure the lid tightly, switch to "manual", set on low pressure, and let cook for 5 minutes.

5. Release pressure, switch back to "sauté", and stir in the cornstarch and water mixture.

6. Let it cook for a few more minutes or until the sauce is thickened.

7. Serve and enjoy.

Southern Fish Fry

Who says that you cannot fry a fish at the multicooker? Well, you can! This Southern Style fried fish is proof. You can pretty much use the multicooker as a deep fryer and fry away just about anything! The trick is to make sure the amount of oil you add into the multicooker is enough to keep the fish from sticking into the sides.

Serving Size: 6

Prep Time: 22 mins

Ingredients:

- 1 ½ lbs. white fish fillets
- ¾ cup breading mix
- 3 tbsp creole mustard
- Freshly ground black pepper to taste
- 1 cup milk
- Juice of 1 pc lemon
- 3 cups vegetable oil

Instructions:

1. Switch the multicooker to "deep fry", then, add oil and let it warm up to 375 degrees F on high.

2. While the oil is heating, mix together mustard, lemon juice, and milk in one bowl.

3. Dip fish in the mustard mixture and coat in breading mix, then, deep fry.

4. Sprinkle freshly ground black pepper on fried fish before serving.

Multicooker Corned Beef

There is nothing a multicooker cannot do. It does not only create delicious recipes wonderfully but do so in a very quick and easy manner. Do you want to serve your family a homemade corned beef? No problem. Switch on your multicooker and make a corned beef meal for the entire family without fuss.

Serving Size: 6

Prep Time: 2 hrs. 45 mins

Ingredients:

- 2 lbs. corned beef brisket
- 1 pc small cabbage head, cored and sliced into wedges
- 1 lb. baby potatoes, halved
- 4 pcs medium carrots, sliced diagonally
- 1 pc large onion, cut into wedges
- 2 tbsp parsley, chopped
- 1oz seasoning packet
- 3 tbsp extra-virgin olive oil
- 4 cups chicken broth
- Kosher salt and freshly ground black pepper to taste

Instructions:

1. Arrange onion wedges at the bottom of the multicooker pot and place the brisket on top.

2. Sprinkle with seasoning mix and pour chicken broth.

3. Secure the lid tightly and set the cooker to "manual" on high pressure, with the timer at 90 minutes.

4. Release the pressure and remove the corned beef, including the onions, and transfer to a bowl, covered with a sheet of aluminum foil to keep warm.

5. Place the remaining veggies into the pot with the cooking liquid, drizzle with olive oil, sprinkle with salt and pepper.

6. Switch back to high pressure and let it cook for the next 5 minutes.

7. Shred the corned beef and serve with cooked veggies on the side.

Multicooker Rotisserie Chicken

So, you are craving for whole roast chicken… Watchugonnado? Well, simply switch on the multicooker and you can have a go on rotisserie chicken at its finest. Here are a few notes, though. First, make sure your chicken is not too big for the cooker. Keep the bird comfortable inside the pot and you will have flavorful and tender chicken in about half an hour. Second, put your choice spices and seasoning as you desired, so you will enjoy every bite.

Serving Size: 8

Prep Time: 30 mins

Ingredients:

- 1-4lbs whole chicken
- 1 tbsp paprika
- ½ tsp dried oregano
- 1 tsp dried thyme
- 1 tsp onion powder
- 2 tsp garlic powder
- 3 tbsp extra virgin olive oil, divided
- 1 cup chicken broth
- 2 tsp salt
- ¼ tsp ground black pepper

Instructions:

1. Mix together the spices in a small bowl until well blended.

2. Massage chicken with two tablespoons of olive oil all over, then, sprinkle with the spice mix and rub from the inside cavity to the loose part between the skin and the meat and through the skin.

3. Switch on the multicooker to "sauté" and heat the remaining oil.

4. Add chicken to the pot, meaty breast side down and let cook for about 5 minutes, then, flip and sear the other side for another 5 minutes.

5. Remove chicken from the pot, pour the chicken broth and let it boil a little, scraping the bottom of the pot to remove the browned bits.

6. Carefully put down a trivet on the pot and place the chicken on top.

7. Close the lid, switch the multicooker to "manual", and let it cook on high pressure for about 24 minutes. If you have a smaller bird, you will need shorter time; if you have a bigger bird, longer time is needed.

8. After 24 minutes, release the pressure, open the lid, and remove the chicken.

9. For extra crispy skin, broil chicken for a few minutes before placing at the serving platter with your favorite side dishes.

10. Serve and enjoy.

Farrotto

Here is another risotto recipe, but we are taking it a healthy level higher. That's because instead of rice, we are using farro, a complicated ancient grain that's composed of varying wheat species. It can be eaten plain, cooked in water until soft, but it is best enjoyed when added into soups and salads.

Serving Size: 4

Prep Time: 30 mins

Ingredients:

- 1 ½ cups farro
- 1 lb. asparagus, trimmed and cut into bite-size pieces
- 1 cup peas
- 1/3 cup Asiago cheese, grated
- 1 pc medium onion, finely chopped
- 2 garlic cloves, chopped
- ¼ cup parsley, chopped
- 2 ¼ cups chicken broth
- Juice of ½ pc lemon
- 1 tbsp unsalted butter
- 3 tbsp water
- ¼ tsp black pepper

Instructions:

1. Switch on the multicooker to "sauté", add water and asparagus and let it cook for about 3 minutes.

2. Drain asparagus and place in a bowl submerged in ice water to stop the cooking process.

3. In the pot, melt butter and sauté onion for about 3 minutes.

4. Stir in farro and garlic and cook for 1 minute more.

5. Pour in broth and stir to blend.

6. Secure the lid and set the multicooker on "high pressure" for 10 minutes.

7. Release the pressure and remove the lid.

8. Add peas and cooked asparagus into the pot to warm through.

9. Turn off the multicooker and fold in cheese, parsley, lemon juice, and salt and pepper into the pot.

10. Stir and serve.

Multicooker BBQ Ribs

Tender-juicy, fall off the bones BBQ Ribs can also be achieved using the multicooker. This version is super saucy and sticky and simply delicious! You can serve it for a weeknight dinner and even for an outdoor barbecue with your family and friends. Given that you have a big enough multicooker, you could make a big batch in less than an hour!

Serving Size: 8

Prep Time: 45 mins

Ingredients:

- 2 racks baby back pork ribs (about 2 lbs. each), trimmed, rinsed, and patted dry
- 2 cups barbecue sauce
- 1 ½ tsp smoked paprika
- 2 tsp ground mustard
- 1 tsp dried thyme
- 1 tsp dried oregano
- ¾ tsp ground cumin
- 2 tsp onion powder
- 1 tsp garlic powder
- 2 tsp chili powder
- ½ tsp cayenne pepper
- 1 tbsp brown sugar
- 2 tsp Kosher salt
- 1 tsp freshly ground black pepper
- ½ cup apple cider vinegar
- 2 cups chicken stock

Instructions:

1. Mix together the dry ingredients composed of spices and seasonings in a bowl.

2. Rub mixture generously onto ribs.

3. Meanwhile, place apple cider vinegar and chicken broth into the multicooker pot, put a trivet on top, and carefully lay the ribs racks on the trivet, wrapping into a coil upright.

4. Set the multicooker to "manual" and cook on high pressure for about 25 minutes. Then, release the pressure to let go of the steam.

5. Preheat the oven to broil and prepare a baking sheet lined with aluminum foil.

6. Place the meat into the baking sheet, meat side up, and generously brush top with barbecue sauce.

7. Broil for about 5 minutes, until caramelized.

8. Serve immediately.

Multicooker Beef Bourguignon

Here is a delicious beef stew made of a wine gravy and tender-juicy beef chunks. This French cuisine's favorite dish can well sit up with the multicooker. And it will not test your patience. You only need a little over an hour to accomplish this delightful, pleasing dinner that your family will love you even more!

Serving Size: 12

Prep Time: 1 hr. 10 mins

Ingredients:

- 3 lbs. beef stew meat, sliced into chunks
- 1 ¾ cups dry red wine
- 8 pcs bacon strips, chopped
- 1 lb. fresh mushrooms, quartered
- 2 cups pearl onions, peeled
- 2 cloves garlic, minced
- 2 tbsp dried parsley
- 3 tbsp dried minced onion
- 1 tsp dried thyme
- 1 pc bay leaf
- 1/3 cup all-purpose flour
- 3 tbsp olive oil
- 1 tsp salt
- ¼ tsp pepper

Instructions:

1. Toss beef with wine, olive oil, dried parsley, dried minced onion, thyme, bay leaf, plus salt and pepper in a large bowl. Cover with a sheet of cling wrap and set aside in the fridge to marinade for 8-12 hours.

2. When beef is ready, switch the multicooker to "sauté" and add chopped bacon. Cook until crispy, stirring often.

3. Remove bacon to a plate using a slotted spoon, then, add mushrooms and onions into the pot. Stir for about 3 minutes.

4. Add garlic and cook for another minute.

5. Stir in beef and bacon, then, sprinkle with flour and toss. Pour the marinade.

6. Secure the lid and turn the switch to "manual" on high pressure for 20 minutes. Release the pressure.

7. Remove the lid and turn back the setting to "sauté" on low to simmer for about 15 minutes until the sauce is thickened.

8. Serve with hot steamed rice or cooked noodles and enjoy.

Chicken Noodle Soup

Chicken noodles do not always have to be an instant thing. But it's not wrong to have it that way, especially when using a multicooker. And it's great, really, because you get all the best of a chicken noodle dish in under an hour.

Serving Size: 6

Prep Time: 50 mins

Ingredients:

- 2 ½ lbs. skinless chicken thighs
- 3 cups wide egg noodles
- 1 ½ cups carrots, peeled and diced
- 1 ½ cup celery stalks, diced
- 1 cup yellow onion, chopped
- 3 tsp garlic, minced
- 2 tsp fresh rosemary, minced
- ¼ cup fresh parsley, chopped
- 2 tsp fresh thyme, minced
- 1 pc bay leaf
- 1 tbsp olive oil
- 1 tbsp fresh lemon juice
- 8 cups chicken broth
- Salt and freshly ground black pepper

Instructions:

1. Set the multicooker on "sauté" and heat on high.

2. Add oil and sauté diced carrots and celery, plus onions.

3. Stir in garlic and cook for 1 more minute.

4. Pour in broth, then, sprinkle rosemary, thyme, and bay leaf. Season with salt and pepper and add chicken.

5. Press "cancel" and close the lid securely.

6. Switch to "manual" and high pressure, then, set the timer to 10 minutes. Release the pressure and remove the chicken from the pot. Transfer to a chopping board and let it cool a little, then, shred the meat using two forks.

7. Meanwhile, switch back the multicooker to "sauté" and add the noodles. Let cook for about 5 minutes or until the noodles are al dente.

8. When the noodles are cooked, put back the chicken into the pot and add lemon juice and parsley.

9. Ladle into serving bowls and serve.

Multicooker Cabbage Rolls

Cabbage Rolls are always a joy to have at the dinner table. It is simply interesting, using cabbage leaves as a wrapper for your beef and rice mix. It's like an entire dinner in one bite. If the cabbage rolls make for an easy meal, preparing it is also no fuss if you are accompanied with a multicooker. Let's start with the recipe!

Serving Size: 6

Prep Time: 3 hrs. 30 mins

Ingredients:

- 1 pc cabbage head
- 1 ½ lbs. ground beef
- 1 ½ cups short-grain rice
- ¾ cups carrots, shredded
- 1 cup onion, diced
- 1 tbsp fresh dill, chopped
- 2 tsp ground mustard
- ½ tsp dried garlic
- 1 tbsp dried green onion
- ¼ cup + 2 tbsp olive oil
- 1 ½ cups chicken broth
- 1 ½ cups water
- 2 tbsp tomato paste
- 1 tbsp garlic powder
- 2 tsp chicken bouillon
- Kosher salt and freshly ground black pepper

Instructions:

1. Separate the cabbage leaves, trimming the core and discarding them, including the veins. Wrap the leaves in plastic wrap and microwave for 3 minutes or until softened.

2. Cut the leaves so they are of almost the same size that can be stuffed with your filling. Set aside.

3. Meanwhile, cook rice by mixing it with water and chicken bouillon in the multicooker. Set to "boil" and the timer to 10 minutes. After 10 minutes, fluff the rice and set aside to cool down.

4. Clean the inner pot of the multicooker and set anew to "sauté" on medium heat.

5. Add ¼ cup of oil and sauté onions until soft and fragrant.

6. Add carrots and stir. Cover and let cook for about 10 minutes, removing the lid and stirring occasionally. Set aside to cool.

7. Combine ground meat, rice, and veggies in a large bowl together with paprika, mustard, dried onion, dried garlic, garlic powder, dill, ½ teaspoon salt, and pepper. Mix until well blended.

8. Prepare the multicooker by arranging several cabbage leaves to cover the bottom of the inner pot.

9. Spoon filling onto the cabbage leaf, fold the sides, and roll to make a burrito. Arrange the cabbage rolls into the pot, seam side down. Repeat until you used up all the ingredients.

10. Meanwhile, stir together chicken broth, tomato paste, and the remaining salt.

11. Pour the liquid onto the pot, drizzle with the remaining 2 tablespoons of oil, and cover with the remaining cabbage leaves.

12. Secure the lid, switch the multicooker to "manual", and set to low pressure for about 35 minutes. Release the pressure and allow the steam to go before opening the lid.

13. Serve and enjoy with your favorite side dish.

Cottage Cheese Pudding

Now, here is an interesting dessert recipe that you can make in your multicooker. It's delightfully good and is so easy to make. You practically will just have to pop everything at the multicooker, wait for a couple of minutes and voila, your dessert is served.

Serving Size: 4

Prep Time: 30 mins

Ingredients:

- 1 lb. cottage cheese
- ½ cup raisins, soaked in water and drained
- 1/3 cup cream of wheat
- 3 pcs eggs, yolks and whites separated
- 1 tbsp butter, melted
- ½ cup sugar
- 1 tsp salt

Instructions:

1. Beat the egg whites and salt until the mixture becomes foamy. Set aside.

2. Meanwhile, mix together cottage cheese, egg yolks, raisins, cream of wheat, and sugar in a large bowl.

3. Slowly beat in egg whites mixture.

4. Grease the inner pot of the multicooker with butter and pour in cottage cheese mix, leveling off the top.

5. Switch on the multicooker to "bake" and set the timer to 25 minutes.

6. Wait for the timer to stop.

7. Serve your pudding with cream and berries if you like.

Corn and Potato Chowder

Here is a comforting chowder that you can make at the multicooker in about 20 minutes. It's rich and creamy and super delicious, loaded with veggies and a tasty soup that will warm up your stomach for sure. This can surely be your next favorite soup, best eaten with crusty bread.

Serving Size: 6

Prep Time: 20 mins

Ingredients:

- 4 pcs corn ears, kernels removed
- 6 pcs red potatoes, diced
- ¼ pc onion, diced
- ¾ cup cheddar cheese
- 3 cups half-and-half
- 3 cups chicken broth
- 2 tbsp corn starch, dissolved in
- 3 tbsp water
- 3 tbsp butter
- Pinch of salt

Instructions:

1. Set the multicooker to "sauté" and heat on medium.

2. Melt butter and sauté onions for about 5 minutes or until softened.

3. Add corn, potatoes, broth, and salt, then, stir to blend.

4. Turn the multicooker onto "manual" and set on high pressure for 10 minutes. Release the pressure and let all the steam gone. Switch back the cooker to "sauté".

5. Gently add cornstarch dissolved in water, stirring constantly until smooth.

6. Stir in half-and-half, plus cheese. Cook until a bit thickened.

7. Serve warm.

Chickpea Curry

Chickpea recipes are a staple in Indian cuisine and this recipe is one of their best. It's an interesting dish, which you can turn completely Vegan and healthy. The secret lies not much on just the chickpeas but the spices. You must have enough Chana Masala in your pantry to be able to make this recipe because that's all that matters. Yes, this dish is fairly spicy but you can't resist its appetizing flare.

Serving Size: 4

Prep Time: 25 mins

Ingredients:

- 12oz dried chickpeas, soaked
- 8oz brown rice, soaked in 2 cups water
- 1 tbsp ginger, peeled and minced
- 1 lb. tomatoes, chopped
- 1 pc red onion, chopped
- 1 tbsp garlic, minced
- 2 tbsp chana masala
- 1 tbsp vegetable oil
- 1 cup water
- 1 tsp sea salt

Instructions:

1. Switch the multicooker on to "sauté".

2. Add oil and let it heat on medium, then, sauté onions for about 5 minutes.

3. Sprinkle spice mix, plus ginger and garlic and continue to stir for another minute.

4. Pour 1 cup of water, plus chickpeas and tomatoes.

5. Place the steamer basket on the inner pot and add the soaked rice placed in a heatproof bowl.

6. Cover and let it steam for 20 minutes.

7. After 20 minutes, set the multicooker to "keep warm" and remove the lid.

8. Stir and adjust seasoning as needed.

9. Serve and enjoy.

Cheesy Egg and Sausage Casserole

Here is a delicious casserole that you can serve for breakfast but you can rightfully enjoy it throughout the day. It's a delicious number made with eggs and flavor-packed sausage, then, made creamy with cheese. Best of all, you can make it in the multicooker without trouble.

Serving Size: 6

Prep Time: 3 hrs. 20 mins

Ingredients:

- 2 cups cheddar cheese, shredded
- 12 pcs large eggs
- 2 cups turkey breakfast sausage, cooked and crumbled
- 32oz hash browns, cubed
- 1 pc large onion, diced
- 1 cup whole milk
- 1 tsp salt
- 1 tsp pepper
- Cooking spray

Instructions:

1. Lightly grease the inner pot of the multicooker with cooking spray.

2. Arrange a layer of hash browns, onions, sausage, and cheese, dividing the ingredients into at least three layers.

3. Whisk together eggs and milk in a bowl, season with salt and pepper and stir.

4. Pour eggs mixture onto the pot, switch the multicooker to "slow cooker" and cook on low for 7 hours. If you need it to be ready faster, cook on high for 3 hours.

5. Serve and enjoy.

Multicooker Korean Beef

Korean Beef is a favorite takeout food for those who love the Asian food flare. But you don't need to takeout anymore. You can make this delicious dish right at home, with the help of your handy multicooker. This dish comes together in less than an hour, making it the perfect choice for a weeknight dinner.

Serving Size: 6

Prep Time: 40 mins

Ingredients:

- 3 lbs. beef chuck roast, cubed
- 4 pcs green onions, thinly sliced
- 6 garlic cloves, minced
- 1 tbsp sesame seeds
- 1/3 cup brown sugar
- 1 tsp dry ground ginger
- 1 tsp onion powder
- 1 tsp black pepper
- ½ cup beef broth
- ½ tbsp rice wine vinegar
- 1/3 cup soy sauce
- 1 tbsp Sriracha sauce
- 3 tbsp cornstarch, dissolved in
- 3 tbsp water

Instructions:

1. Combine beef with the rest of the ingredients on the inner pot of the multicooker, except for the cornstarch-water mixture, green onions, and sesame seeds. Stir to blend.

2. Secure the lid and set to "manual" on high pressure, with the timer at 30 minutes. Then, release the pressure until all the steam is gone.

3. Open the lid, stir in the cornstarch slurry, and switch the multicooker to "sauté". Let the sauce thicken for about 3 minutes.

4. Serve with a garnish of freshly chopped green onions and sesame seeds over hot steamed rice.

Beef and Mushroom Stew

Craving for a beef dinner, but you do not have the whole day to tenderize a tough beef cut? Well, the multicooker is your friend. It will allow you the best beef stew with whatever ingredient you might dish out and turn it into an excitingly delicious meal.

Serving Size: 6

Prep Time: 40 mins

Ingredients:

- 2 lbs. beef chuck, cubed
- 1oz dried porcini mushrooms, soaked and chopped
- 2 pcs large carrots, sliced into 1/2-inch rounds
- 1 pc celery stalk, sliced
- 1 pc rosemary sprig, finely chopped
- 1 pc medium red onion, diced
- ½ cup red wine
- 1 cup beef stock
- 1 tbsp olive oil
- 2 tbsp unsalted butter
- 2 tbsp all-purpose flour
- 1 tsp salt
- ¼ tsp pepper

Instructions:

1. Switch the multicooker to "sauté" and let it heat on medium.

2. Add oil and brown beef cubes for about 5 minutes.

3. Stir in onions, celery, rosemary, vinegar, and beef stock. Sprinkle with salt and pepper and mix well.

4. Add carrots and mushrooms into the pot, close the lid, and switch to "manual".

5. Cook on high pressure with the timer set to 15 minutes. Then, release the pressure until all the steam is gone.

6. Meanwhile, melt butter in a saucepan over medium fire and sprinkle flour, stir until the mixture turns into a paste.

7. When the multicooker timer is up, switch back to "sauté", lift the lid, and ladle some soup into the pan with butter and flour. Mix well and then, pour back into the multicooker.

8. Stir the stew and let cook for another few minutes until the sauce is thick.

9. Serve with rice or mashed potatoes.

Multicooker Fish Mix

Here is something interesting for you and your multicooker. It's a mix of fish fillets cooked in cheese and cream. Wonder what it tastes like? Well, this is your opportunity to stop wondering and actually tasting. Make this recipe in less than half an hour and see how it pleases your diners instantly.

Serving Size: 4

Prep Time: 20 mins

Ingredients:

- ½ lb. tilapia fillet, cubed
- ½ lb. salmon fillet, cubed
- 1 cup cheddar cheese, shredded
- 1 cup all-purpose cream
- ½ tsp dried oregano
- ½ tsp garlic powder
- ½ tsp cayenne pepper
- Salt and pepper to taste

Instructions:

1. Combine all the ingredients on the inner pot of your multicooker and stir. Place cheese on top to cover the rest.

2. Secure the lid and switch to "multicooker" for 20 minutes.

3. Serve and enjoy.

Multicooker Spaghetti

Did we mention that the multicooker can offer endless pasta-abilities? Oh yes, it's true. It's one of the best places to cook pasta because you will not need to precook anything. Just throw all the ingredients into the multicooker, raw pasta included, and come up with the same delicious pasta dish you have been craving for.

Serving Size: 4

Prep Time: 40 mins

Ingredients:

- 8oz spaghetti
- 1 lb. ground beef
- 2 pc medium carrots, peeled and finely chopped
- 1-28oz can crushed tomatoes
- 3 pcs celery stalks, finely chopped
- 1 pc medium yellow onion, finely chopped
- 2 garlic cloves, finely chopped
- 1 cup Parmesan cheese, shredded
- 1 tsp dried oregano
- 1 tsp crushed red pepper flakes
- ½ cup dry red wine
- 2 cups chicken stock
- 2 tbsp olive oil
- Salt and pepper to taste

Instructions:

1. Switch the multicooker to "sauté" and heat olive oil on medium.

2. Add ground meat, stirring often and breaking apart with the back of the spoon, until seared.

3. Stir in carrots, celery, onions, and garlic. Sprinkle oregano, red pepper flakes, salt, and pepper.

4. Pour in wine and let it simmer, scraping the bits at the bottom, for about 5 minutes.

5. Add tomatoes and chicken stock.

6. Break apart the spaghetti noodles by half and throw into the pot, stirring to keep the noodles from sticking at the bottom of the inner pot.

7. Turn the dial to "pressure cook" on high and set the timer to 8 minutes. Then, release the pressure.

8. Switch to "keep warm" and let it cook for a few more minutes.

9. Stir and serve with freshly grated cheese.

Multicooker Pork Chops

Here is a delicious pork chop dinner that you can make in the multicooker. It's quick and easy with a very simple flavor profile. It's easy to love and will surely make mealtime fun for everyone, including the young ones.

Serving Size: 4

Prep Time: 40 mins

Ingredients:

- 4 pcs boneless pork chops
- 2 pcs large yellow onions, thinly sliced
- 2 tbsp sour cream
- 4 tbsp unsalted butter
- 1 cup chicken broth
- ½ cup all-purpose flour
- 1 tsp Kosher salt
- ½ tsp freshly ground black pepper

Instructions:

1. Sprinkle salt and pepper onto pork chops, coat in flour.

2. Switch on the multi-cooker to "sauté" and melt butter on high heat.

3. Working in batches, brown coated chops for about 5 minutes total, flipping once.

4. Transfer pork chops to a plate and keep warm.

5. Meanwhile, sauté onions into the multicooker for 10 minutes or until caramelized.

6. Add chicken broth and let it simmer, scraping the bottom with any browned bits.

7. Put back the pork chops, switch to "manual" and cook on high pressure for 10 minutes. Then, release the pressure until all the steam is gone.

8. Open the lid, switch back to "sauté" and let it cook for a few minutes more or until the sauce is thickened.

9. Serve and enjoy.

Garlicky Pot Roast

For the final recipe that will make you put your multicooker into good use, here is a classic pot roast that's oozing with flavors. It can be eaten with rice and other side dishes or serve it with buns and you will love the result. The meat is so tender and flavorful that you will keep asking for more.

Serving Size: 6

Prep Time: 4 hrs. 15 mins

Ingredients:

- 2 pcs carrots, peeled
- 1 pc onion, peeled
- 1 pc large yellow onion, sliced into rings
- 3 garlic cloves, minced
- 2 tbsp olive oil
- ¼ cup green onion, chopped
- 3 tbsp parsley, chopped
- 3 tbsp BBQ sauce
- 3 cups beef broth
- 2 pcs bay leaves
- 1 tsp mustard seeds
- 1 tbsp Kosher salt
- 1 tsp black peppercorns
- 4 lbs. beef chuck roast, cubed
- Pinch of red pepper flakes

Instructions:

1. Combine beef and broth in a multicooker, set into "slow cook" and the timer to 3 hours with the lid on.

2. Open the lid, then, add the whole carrots and onions, plus mustard seeds, bay leaves, salt, and peppercorns. Cook for another hour. Remove the meat to a chopping board and let cool. Shred using two forks.

3. Meanwhile, heat oil in a pan and sauté the onions until caramelized.

4. Take about 1 cup of liquid through a fine sieve, discarding solids.

5. When ready to serve, place shredded meat in a serving bowl, toss with caramelized onions and fresh garlic, then, garnish with chopped green onions and parsley. Drizzle with reserved liquid and BBQ sauce.

6. Serve and enjoy.

Conclusion

Multicookers are super-efficient. They are worth the investment for providing convenience around the kitchen. It allows you to perform different cooking tasks so as to enjoy a handful of different recipes each time. Your recipe calls for boiling, steaming, sautéing, deep-frying, roasting, or stewing? No problem, because this single appliance could cover all those.

This multicooker cookbook is intended to introduce you to the multi-benefits this kitchen counter must-have could offer. We want to get you started on putting the unit into good use and do so while giving your family the most delectable meals they deserve. These multicooker recipes can well be altered and cook the traditional way. But if you made the multicooker investment, who cares about conventional cooking?

Upon browsing through the recipes gathered in this cookbook, you will be surprised at how functional this small unit appliance could become. It is the best partner for novice cooks so they can come up with even the most complicated recipes by simply pushing a couple of buttons. It is such a huge bonus that the multicooker operates amazingly well with well-loved family meals as well as gourmet recipes you would dare come up with when some occasion calls for them.

This cookbook is your way of making good use of the multicooker and rightfully so because after mastering its use, you can confidently prepare anything. And take note, multicooker recipes come out incredibly moist, tender-juicy, and overall appetizing. Your family will be constantly pleased!

Happy cooking!

About the Author

Molly Mills always knew she wanted to feed people delicious food for a living. Being the oldest child with three younger brothers, Molly learned to prepare meals at an early age to help out her busy parents. She just seemed to know what spice went with which meat and how to make sauces that would dress up the blandest of pastas. Her creativity in the kitchen was a blessing to a family where money was tight and making new meals every day was a challenge.

Molly was also a gifted athlete as well as chef and secured a Lacrosse scholarship to Syracuse University. This was a blessing to her family as she was the first to go to college and at little cost to her parents. She took full advantage of her college education and earned a business degree. When she graduated, she joined her culinary skills and business acumen into a successful catering business. She wrote her first e-book after a customer asked if she could pay for several of her recipes. This sparked the entrepreneurial spirit in Mills and she thought if one person wanted them, then why not share the recipes with the world!

Molly lives near her family's home with her husband and three children and still cooks for her family every chance she gets. She plays Lacrosse with a local team made up of her old teammates from college and there are always some tasty nibbles on the ready after each game.

Don't Miss Out!

Scan the QR-Code below and you can sign up to receive emails whenever Molly Mills publishes a new book. There's no charge and no obligation.

Sign Me Up

https://molly.gr8.com

Printed in Great Britain
by Amazon